T0228840

# TWO STEP

Rhashan Stone
# TWO STEP

OBERON BOOKS

LONDON

First published in 2004 by Oberon Books Ltd
521 Caledonian Road, London N7 9RH
Tel: 020 7607 3637 / Fax: 020 7607 3629
e-mail: oberon.books@btinternet.com
www.oberonbooks.com

A catalogue record for this book is available from the British Library.

ISBN: 1 84002 501 8

Cover image by Lara Platman

# Characters

MONA

LENNY

HETTIE

AJ

*Two Step* was first performed at the Almeida Theatre on 30 August 2004, with the following cast:

MONA, Doña Croll
LENNY, Derek Griffiths
HETTIE, Remi Wilson
AJ, Ricci McLeod

Director, Josette Bushell-Mingo
Set and costume design, Bernadette Roberts
Lighting design, Phil Gladwell
Sound design, Cormac O'Connor

*Two Step* was commissioned by Push 04 and the Almeida Theatre.

*'All cruelty springs from weakness.'*
(Seneca 4BC–AD65)

# Prologue

*The door slams. MONA, an attractive black woman, late fifties, stands against the door breathing heavily, clearly agitated. She allows the shopping bags to drop to the floor and she reaches for a handkerchief to wipe her brow.*

MONA: I won't let you. Not this time.

*She scrambles for her keys and triple locks the door before going to the window, checking that the curtains are fully closed.*

MONA: Not this time.

*She goes back to the front door where the shopping bags lie. She goes to pick them up. A sudden knock at the door. MONA freezes. Another knock at the door. MONA doesn't dare move.*

*Silence.*

*A sudden peal of laughter. The laugh of a small child.*

MONA: You shouldn't be here. I told you. You have to go.

*The child's voice is heard crying, softly.*

MONA: I can't bear it when you – Please don't. Please – You shouldn't be here.

*Suddenly – a banging. MONA is terrified. She presses her back against the door, shaking with fear. The banging continues, louder now. MONA covers her mouth with her hands, suppressing a scream. She can't contain it any longer.*

MONA: Leave me alone! I don't want you!

*The banging continues, the sound becoming increasingly distorted until –*

# Scene One

*A council flat in Battersea. MONA sits at the dining table. She is the picture of composure as she sits opposite LENNY, an attractive black man of a similar age. He is wearing a casual linen suit and smart brown loafers. MONA has prepared tea –*

LENNY: People don't walk anywhere anymore do they? It's just not done. Particularly Americans.

*Pause.*

Funny that.

*MONA lifts the lid of the teapot to see if it has brewed to her satisfaction. It hasn't.*

A watched pot never brews, eh?

*Pause.*

You can't go wrong with a good cup of tea.

*Beat.*

Well, actually you can. My mother was always a 'warm the pot first' woman and I have to say I agree. And it's nice to see you still using a pot. Most people just make it in the cup.

*Pause.*

And then there are those who put the milk in first. Apparently it stops you getting that greasy film you can sometimes get on top. Downside is, it clogs up the paper and the flavour gets locked inside. Oh, and you should never pour boiling water straight onto the bag. Scorches the paper and leaves a funny aftertaste.

*Beat.*

Apparently.

*Silence. MONA scrutinizes LENNY.*

What?

MONA: You look –

LENNY: The same?

MONA: Well –

LENNY: Yes?

MONA: No.

LENNY: No?

MONA: No. I hardly recognize you.

LENNY: Oh.

*Pause.*

So. How have you…

MONA: Managed?

LENNY: Been. How have you –

MONA: Fine.

LENNY: Good.

MONA: You?

LENNY: Great. Fantastic.

MONA: Really?

LENNY: Really.

MONA: Oh. That's nice.

*MONA checks the teapot. Satisfied she begins to pour –*

LENNY: You look –

MONA: Different?

LENNY: Older. No – that's not what I meant.

MONA: What did you mean?

LENNY: Mature. Rounded. Not your figure, obviously –
More that you've…grown into yourself.

*Beat.*

More.

MONA: Sugar?

LENNY: Yes. I mean no. Sorry. I forgot I'm supposed to be
watching the weight. Is it me or is it hot in here?

MONA: It's you. Milk?

LENNY: Thank you.

*MONA heaps a teaspoon of powdered milk into LENNY's
cup. He looks on appalled.*

As I was saying you look –

MONA: Older?

LENNY: No. More… Well what I meant was.

MONA: Lenny. I think we've covered this subject already.
Don't you?

LENNY: Yes. I suppose we have.

*LENNY sips his tea.*

Who'da thought?

MONA: Yes. Who'da thought.

LENNY: I really can't tell you how good it is to see you
again.

MONA: I really can't tell you either.

*Pause.*

What have you done with your voice?

LENNY: Excuse me?

MONA: Your voice. It's changed.

LENNY: Has it? No. Yes. A little, maybe. I don't know. I'm a writer.

MONA: A writer.

LENNY: Yes.

MONA: So that's how writers talking these days?

LENNY: I went back to college. To study English.

MONA: You already speak English what else is there to learn?

LENNY: Well it just goes to show that you can teach an old dog new tricks.

MONA: And what kind of college take an old dog like you?

LENNY: North London College. Right on the doorstep.

MONA: Well isn't that – convenient. So what did you learn while you was studying English sitting on the doorstep at North London College?

LENNY: I always wanted to write a book actually, stretch myself creatively. I wanted to explore certain aspects of my personality that had been lying dormant for years.

MONA: Like?

LENNY: Oh. Well. You know.

*Pause.*

So in answer to your question, the learning continues. One should really see oneself as a student of Life.

MONA: I see.

*Beat.*

So where is one living now?

LENNY: Islington.

MONA: Islington?

LENNY: Yes. Islington.

MONA: Flat?

LENNY: House.

MONA: Nice. Still work for the Council?

LENNY: No. As I said –

MONA: College. Yes. Of course. I remember. A writer. You stay out of trouble these days?

LENNY: Trouble? Me? Hardly.

*The sound of breaking glass from outside. A voice calls out.*

LENNY: You think my car's alright out there?

MONA: Depends on how nice your car is.

LENNY: Right. Well, I won't stay long. As I said. I was just passing.

MONA: Time to see a man about a dog?

LENNY: Huh? Oh I see. Very funny. Yes. I mean, no. No men with dogs for me. With age comes responsibility.

MONA: Not even the occasional flutter?

LENNY: Those days are behind me. I don't need those things anymore. I'm settled.

MONA: Settled?

LENNY: Married.

MONA: Married?

LENNY: Married. Yes.

MONA: That's. Nice.

*LENNY goes to his jacket pocket and begins fishing around.*

I'll get you an ashtray.

LENNY: No. I wasn't – I don't. Not anymore.

MONA: Since when?

LENNY: Ages. No I was looking for a picture. Must be in my other wallet.

MONA: I have that problem too. 'Where oh where did I put my other purse. The one with all the money in.'

*LENNY laughs. MONA doesn't.*

So. Married. You still on best behaviour, or she find out what you really like yet?

LENNY: Things are different now. She understands me.

MONA: Every woman understand man alright. We understand perfectly well. What she don't know won't hurt her, huh?

LENNY: I'd never cheat on Susan.

MONA: Just me?

LENNY: We weren't married.

MONA: Yes, that does make a difference. Having it written down. Something official to remind you not to go out sniffing around other people's trash cans. But then again you always were –

LENNY: What?

MONA: Nothing. I'm sure things must be different now for you and – ?

LENNY: Susan.

MONA: Susan.

LENNY: Susan. Yes.

MONA: Nice name.

LENNY: Nice woman.

*Pause.*

MONA: It's Saturday night. A bit of action? A few drinks? I know you.

LENNY: Not anymore.

MONA: You were always after something, Lenny. I reckon you got a little something cooking on the stove.

LENNY: No.

MONA: A little piece o' chicken sizzling away down here in South London. All you have to do is pop down here and check the seasoning every now and again.

LENNY: As I said. I was just passing.

MONA: Since when you pass Battersea fe reach Islington?

LENNY: I love my wife.

MONA: I didn't ask if you love her I asked if you're faithful to her? Surely as a man you know there's a difference?

LENNY: Surely as a woman you know not to ask.

MONA: After 32 years you come to my house, out of the blue, uninvited, smelling like Kew Gardens and chatting to me like I just step off the boat. Don't forget I know you. I know you're in there. Behind your new clothes, your new hair, your new teeth. I always say 'Never trust a man wid bad teeth. Rotten teeth. Rotten man.'

LENNY: What's wrong with my teeth?

MONA: They're false.

LENNY: They're mine. I paid for them.

MONA: With what? You have job?

LENNY: No –

MONA: No?

LENNY: No. Once I get my degree –

MONA: Ah –

LENNY: Ah?

MONA: Ah – So Susan have money?

LENNY: Susan has a job if that's what you mean.

MONA: No. That's not what I mean. What I mean is – and I'm sorry if I'm not making myself clear – Is Susan working hard every day to pay the bills and put a roof over your head while you sit around on your backside all day living the life of a student? If she is, then it seems to me she at least deserves to have a husband who is faithful. As a kept man, surely you understand that's not too much to ask?

LENNY: Things change.

*MONA kisses her teeth.*

It's the truth.

MONA: Once a cheat, always a cheat. She's a fool if she thinks otherwise.

LENNY: She's not a fool. She's been to University.

MONA: Then she's a fool with a degree.

*Pause.*

So tell me more about this white Susan from the University.

LENNY: What makes you think she's white?

MONA: Lenny. How many black woman you know named Susan? But then again, maybe you have them where you live. In Islington.

*Beat.*

You have black people where you live?

LENNY: It's Islington, Mona. Not Hampstead.

MONA: You have black friends? I mean, that you actually let in her house.

LENNY: Last time I checked.

MONA: And Susan alright with that?

LENNY: If she isn't, she hides it well.

MONA: Yes. Well, that's white folks for you.

LENNY: And a full house is a happy house don't you think? It's hard to keep up with our social commitments sometimes I must admit. You must know that feeling? Mind you here you are all tucked up on a Saturday night. Edging over to the slow lane, eh Mona?

MONA: I've had a busy week. –

LENNY: Good for you. At least living on your own means you don't have people in and out of your house all day and night. AJ's friends seem to live with us more than they do with their own parents.

MONA: Who's AJ?

LENNY: Thank God for takeaway delivery service, that's what I say. A couple of large pizzas and a DVD and we don't hear a peep out of him for days.

MONA: Out of who?

LENNY: My son.

*MONA stiffens.*

Didn't I mention him?

MONA: No. You didn't.

LENNY: That's a first. I usually bore the pants off anyone who will listen. Top of his class. An excellent sportsman, academically gifted, musical – I could go on.

MONA: Don't on my account.

LENNY: How lucky am I? And a son. Bang. First time. Just like that.

MONA: An only child though? Must be difficult?

LENNY: No.

MONA: No?

LENNY: No.

MONA: Oh.

*Beat.*

LENNY: Susan would like another. She's certainly still young enough. Me? I'm not so sure. Depends on the window of opportunity. You?

MONA: Me what?

LENNY: Did you ever…?

MONA: No.

*Beat.*

LENNY: Didn't…fancy it?

MONA: By the time you left, by the time I got over it…
Well, let's just say that my window of opportunity had
already closed firmly behind me. But it's wonderful to
see that yours is still swinging open after all these years.
As you said 'Lucky you'. Congratulations.

*Pause.*

So how old is this Susan?

LENNY: How old? Or how young?

*Beat.*

This is extraordinary. Who would have thought after all
this time?

MONA: Yes. Who'da thought?

LENNY: I meant what I said earlier. I really can't tell you
how good it is to see you again.

MONA: And I meant it when I said I really can't either.

*MONA gets up and goes towards the kitchen.*

LENNY: Where are you going?

MONA: Sun's over the yardarm. As if you hadn't noticed.

LENNY: I really shouldn't stay too long.

MONA: There is a God.

*MONA exits. LENNY immediately takes a handkerchief from
his pocket, wipes his brow and takes three deep breaths. MONA
re-enters with two glasses and some ice.*

MONA: What'll you have?

LENNY: Coke if you have it.

MONA: With?

LENNY: Ice?

MONA: I still buy good whiskey you know, no need to turn your nose up.

LENNY: I don't drink anymore.

MONA: Excuse me?

LENNY: I'm in recovery.

MONA: From what?

LENNY: From being an alcoholic.

*MONA screams with laughter. LENNY doesn't.*

LENNY: What's so funny?

MONA: All those years drinking must a' really licked you if you still recovering from it now.

LENNY: That's one way of putting it.

MONA: Well I'm not surprised. Nobody could put away as much as you did. Nobody. Best thing for a hangover? Hair of the dog.

LENNY: I don't drink.

MONA: So you said.

*Beat.*

What about birthdays?

LENNY: No.

MONA: A little sherry at Christmas?

LENNY: No, nothing. 'One drink. One drunk.' Besides, it's against the rules.

MONA: Whose rules?

> *Beat.*

> AA? You?

LENNY: I'm full of surprises.

MONA: But they so strict.

LENNY: Yes, Mona, that's the point. It's changed my life. My book is inspired by the whole experience.

MONA: Sound rough to me. You have to do them…?

LENNY: Steps?

MONA: Steps.

LENNY: Yes.

MONA: How many are there?

LENNY: Twelve.

MONA: And how many you do?

LENNY: Eight.

MONA: Eight?

LENNY: Eight. So far.

MONA: Typical. You never finish anything.

LENNY: It's a journey, and journeys never end.

MONA: But you writing a book about it! How can they let you write a book about The Twelve Steps and you only reach Eight? I should write a book called *How To Live To A Hundred And Three*. I'm only fifty but, hey, what does that matter?

LENNY: Only?

MONA: Only…just.

LENNY: I think you understand the process.

MONA: I don't need to. You're the one with the problem.

LENNY: Correct. And oh, how I envy your perfect life. Step One. I admitted that I was powerless, in my case over alcohol, and that my life had become unmanageable.

MONA: Meaning?

LENNY: Meaning. Yes, you're quite right. There is meaning in everything.

*Beat.*

The only book I need, the only instruction manual I need for living a rich life are The Twelve Steps. If I live by these rules one day at a time I will find peace and serenity within myself. Just like you, Mona.

MONA: Well I must say you certainly have changed. House. Car. Children. Married. Faithful, apparently. New clothes. New voice. New teeth. And sober. At least you still black I suppose that's one blessing. Mind you...

LENNY: Mind what?

MONA: Roots are so important don't you think? I mean, look what 'appen to Michael Jackson. Been around all dem la-di-da folk so long, him forget he black. Now him want the outside to match the inside. Not that I'm saying you're anywhere near as bad as him yet, but I'd hate for you to forget who you really are.

LENNY: With so many people around to remind me, how could I forget?

MONA: There are a lot of people we knew that would find your transformation a little –

LENNY: Like who?

MONA: No-one in particular. Just folk.

LENNY: Like who? Who do you still see?

MONA: Does it matter?

LENNY: I'm interested. Come on, throw some names at me.

*Beat.*

Me? I never kept in touch with anyone. But you? You were always so good at all that. And it's good to see that you still keep yourself active.

*Beat.*

So. Who?

MONA: I was illustrating a point.

LENNY: Jerome? You still see him?

MONA: No.

LENNY: Why?

MONA: Because I never like him that's why. Shifty eyes.

LENNY: That Jamaican with the flat feet?

MONA: Who?

LENNY: Good dancer. Flat feet. You see him?

MONA: No.

LENNY: Why?

MONA: Because he's dead. Or living in an old people's home in Tower Hamlets, same thing. Why you asking me about flat footed Jamaicans and people I don't like?

LENNY: I just want to know who you still see. I'm interested to know which people you were talking about when you said that they would be interested in my 'transformation'.

*Pause.*

MONA: Billy James.

LENNY: Who?

MONA: You remember. Tall African guy.

LENNY: Can you narrow it down a bit?

MONA: You know who I mean. You always got on so well.

LENNY: African you say?

MONA: Did security sometimes at the Mayflower hotel. Let me see now. I think he might have been, yes I'm sure he was, a friend of Gloria's.

*Beat.*

LENNY: Gloria?

MONA: Gloria Pittman. Friend of.

LENNY: I didn't meet any of Gloria's friends.

MONA: Oh. My mistake.

*Pause.*

You still see Gloria?

LENNY: (*Quickly.*) No. You?

MONA: Not recently. I'm surprised. You –

LENNY: Why would I still see Gloria? We were never close.

MONA: Just close enough, eh. Last time I saw her she looked way past her sell-by date. Face like a slapped arse.

LENNY: Well, none of us is getting any younger, Mona.

MONA: Meaning?

LENNY: Meaning. Yes. There is meaning in everything.

*Beat.*

MONA: Not a very good dancer, Gloria. Too busty. Unstable ballast. I can't think what you saw in her.

LENNY: I don't remember. She was there.

MONA: How romantic.

LENNY: It was never that. I was drunk.

MONA: You were always drunk. How many times?

LENNY: Does it matter?

MONA: Yes. I know you slept with her after I –

LENNY: (*Quickly.*) You knew who I was. What kind of man.

MONA: I soon learnt. The kind of man that jumps into bed with another woman when his girlfriend has just –

LENNY: I don't think you're in any position to throw stones, Mona.

MONA: I hope it still keeps you awake at night –

LENNY: My conscience is clear.

MONA: Because the alcohol washed it away.

LENNY: I'm an adult. I'm not answerable to you.

MONA: Then who?

LENNY: God knows –

MONA: So you believe in God now too?

LENNY: God knows –

MONA: Yes, God knows. He truly knows and if I were you, like the shepherds keeping watch over their flocks by night, I would be sore afraid.

LENNY: Step Two. I came to believe that a Power greater than myself could restore me to sanity.

MONA: Coming in here –

LENNY: Step Three. I made a decision to turn my will and my life over to God, as I –

MONA: Too late, Lenny –

LENNY: It's never too –

MONA: Coming in here talkin like a wh –

LENNY: What?

MONA: Yeah, you heard it. Look at you. You can read all their books. You can marry their women. You can live in their houses and drive their cars. But you still black, Lenny. Everybody else know it, 'cos they can see it. You don't even know the shame you bringing on yourself when you come in here, in my house, the woman who knew you from time. So. You may not have heard me the first time so I gonna say it again so you can hear it clearly. Shamin' yourself by talkin' like a wh –

LENNY: Don't. Finish. That –

MONA: Or what?

*LENNY takes three long, deep breaths.*

LENNY: I have to tell you at this point that you're making me feel uncomfortable. I don't know what it is that you want me to say because I'm getting such conflicting signals. I sense that you want to draw me into some kind of conflict but I'm afraid I'm going to have to resist that. It's just not working for me. I'm sorry if that makes you feel awkward. Or unhappy. I got drunk and I slept with Gloria. I can say that now as a fully present adult. I acknowledged that and I moved on. I don't need to be told that it was wrong. I already know. But I was –

MONA: Powerless?

LENNY: Step Four. I made a searching and fearless moral inventory of myself –

MONA: So you must have asked yourself why you did it?

LENNY: I don't know why, because I was drunk. I can't remember anything more about it, because I was drunk. I couldn't control what was happening to me, because I was drunk.

MONA: So the drink *made* you do it. Or maybe Gloria *made* you do it? God forbid it should actually be your fault. Next thing you'll be telling me that I drove you to do it.

*LENNY shrugs.*

LENNY: 'One day at a time. Here and now. I can't change yesterday. Tomorrow is still unknown. Only today.'

*Beat.*

I don't want to lay the finger of blame here but I say this without anger, hostility or resentment. You took me as a drinker. There was no deception. All this is about the fact that it's hard for you to accept me as a *non* drinker. But. The Universe will provide.

MONA: You mean Susan will provide.

*MONA stands up and makes her way to the kitchen.*

LENNY: Where are you going?

MONA: To get you that coke. Unless, of course, the Universe is gonna get it.

*As MONA exits LENNY checks his watch. He crosses to the window and opens the curtains. Under the curtains are a set of Venetian blinds which he also draws, revealing wooden shutters. LENNY closes the curtains again.*

LENNY: (*To himself.*) The Universe will provide.

*LENNY crosses to the door and attempts to work out how to get the many locks undone. He succeeds and opens the door, then leans against the doorframe looking out. The sound of a toilet flushing off. MONA enters with a coke.*

Better?

*MONA doesn't move. She falters –*

Mona?

MONA: Why did you do that?

LENNY: I just thought –

MONA: What are you doing?

LENNY: Clear the air.

MONA: I can breathe just fine with the door closed. Come away.

LENNY: Got enough locks on the door?

MONA: It keeps them out.

LENNY: Or you in.

MONA: Don't they have crime where you live?

LENNY: What? You think you're any safer just because the door is closed?

*Beat.*

Something in the air. Can you smell it?

MONA: The bin men don't come till Tuesday.

LENNY: It's been raining. I love the smell of London after rain. Don't you like to be outside?

MONA: What's so good about outside? I've seen it all before.

LENNY: If I thought that I'd just roll over and give it all up now. What a beautiful night. Of course with the light that's produced in cities now it's difficult to see the night sky properly. Where we live it's a little clearer. On nights like this when I'm walking home I put my head right back and look straight up into the sky so I can't see land or trees or anything.

MONA: You should be careful. Might get run over.

LENNY: I feel as if I could pass out sometimes when I think how big it all is.

MONA: Now you're just bragging.

LENNY: Don't you take anything seriously anymore?

MONA: Things that are serious. Yes.

LENNY: What could be more serious than hurtling through the cosmos on this big old hunk of rock?

*Suddenly-*

There! Look!

MONA: (*Startled.*) What?

LENNY: A shooting star. And you missed it.

MONA: Jesus, Lenny, you scared the life out of me.

LENNY: 'Twinkle, twinkle little star. How I wonder what you are.' The Higher Power speaks with a quiet voice.

MONA: I wish you would.

LENNY: Amazing. Just amazing. It's all exactly as it should be. The Universe in harmony with itself. Me. You. Here. A shooting star. Just when you think you're in control, just when you begin taking it for granted – a message comes. You just have to be ready for it.

*A peal of laughter from outside. The laugh of a small child.*

MONA: Lenny. Can you close the door now? Please.

LENNY: Why? What are you scared of?

MONA: I'm not scared of anything. That bloody draught is aggravating my arthritis.

LENNY: You're being facetious. It takes millions of light years for that light to reach us. Can you even begin to comprehend that? Millions of light years later my eye happens to flick upwards. But by the time we see it, by the time we *get* it, it isn't even there anymore. It's dead. Gone. I can't take something like that in my stride. Don't you see? We know it. But we don't *get* it. We miss…the wonder. We want to get to the destination more than we want to go on the journey. All we want is the answer. But that's the easy bit. Switch on. Log in. Enter. Then when we've found it – which usually takes about 30 seconds on the internet depending on what you're looking for and how fast your modem is – Then, when we find it, it loses its magic. It becomes ordinary. We should always wonder. Always think 'that's amazing'. It's as good a reason as any to keep going. That's why I carry on. That's why I keep searching, growing. As soon as I open my eyes in the morning I say to myself 'Hallelujah! I'm still here. Despite everything. I'm still here.' I mean – if light from a distant planet can take millions upon millions of light years to cross the galaxy for God knows what reason – I sure as hell can get out of bed in the morning.

MONA: What do you mean, facetious?

LENNY: There it is again. What's happened to you?

MONA: To me? What's happened to me?

LENNY: We used to have fun.

MONA: *We* used to be *we*. We aren't *we* anymore.

LENNY: We could at least enjoy each other's company.

MONA: And what makes you think I'm not?

LENNY: Because your face looks like you're chewing on a bee.

MONA: Well. Looks can be deceiving. Can't they Leonard?

LENNY: Things aren't as bad as you're afraid they might be. Or want them to be.

MONA: Excuse me?

LENNY: You're afraid. And that's OK. It's just where you are right now.

MONA: I know exactly where I am you self-righteous son-of-a-bitch. And you're looking at it. I'm in the real world. The world that's here in front of me and the world that's always right behind me no matter how fast I run. I'm not afraid, Lenny. I'm fed up. Fed up with you sitting here in my house trying to pluck up the courage to ask me whatever is that you need to ask me. I know that you didn't come here to pass the time of day. You want something from me. You've always wanted something from me.

*Pause.*

I'm not afraid.

*Pause.*

The only reason I have to be afraid is because you come to my house after dark and leave the bloody door open. Anybody could walk in, and what you gonna do then? With your old hips and brittle bones? Aggravating my head with your New Age nonsense. Aggravating my arthritis with your… I'm not afraid, Lenny. I'm angry and I want a drink.

*Pause.*

Haven't you got a home to go to? Oh look! The moon is shifting in the heavens. Its a sign. It means that all aged, slack-hipped, fake tooth, black men, that have nothing better to do than chat nonsense, should get in their cars and go back to their skinny, young, flat-titty wives who are waiting at home for them with a cup of Horlicks and the *Telegraph.* Unless, of course, they have something they wish to say?

LENNY: Why so angry?

MONA: You never heard the old saying? Retaliate first.

*LENNY begins to collect up his things.*

LENNY: 'God grant me the serenity to accept the things I cannot change; the courage to change the things I can; and the wisdom to know the difference.'

*LENNY and MONA stand facing each other, neither willing to make the next move. LENNY takes a step towards MONA before changing his mind. He exits, thinks about closing the door behind him but decides to leave it open.*

MONA: Son-of-a –

*The sound of footsteps approaching the door. They stop in the street outside. Silence.*

Lenny?

*A shadow passes in the street outside. It is the silhouette of a young woman. A peal of laughter.*

No!

*MONA rushes to the door and triple locks it.*

And stay out.

*A peel of laughter echoes in the room. The laugh of a small child. MONA turns to find HETTIE facing her across the room, soaked to the skin. MONA freezes.*

You can't be here. You can't.

HETTIE: Ssh...

MONA: This cannot be.

*HETTIE touches her stomach lightly.*

HETTIE: Ssh...

*MONA touches her stomach lightly.*

MONA: Ssh...

*HETTIE slaps her stomach with one swift, sharp movement. MONA clutches her stomach in pain.*

Lenny!

*Silence.*

HETTIE: You should have let me go.

MONA: I tried.

*HETTIE touches her forehead.*

HETTIE: In here?

MONA: Look at you. I always imagined...

HETTIE: Heart dried, worn hollow
Yellow bile too thick to swallow.
You called. I came.
You lead. I follow.

*HETTIE moves towards MONA.*

MONA: No. You can't stay here. I told you, you have to –

*HETTIE extends her arm slowly, deliberately, and places her hand over MONA's heart. A moment, then MONA recoils in horror.*

It's cold.

# Scene Two

*The following day –*

*LENNY stands facing MONA who is wearing a dressing gown. She looks terrible.*

LENNY: I felt that there was a lot of negative energy surrounding us yesterday. Our meeting. Not surprising really, considering. But the main thing is we shouldn't feel bad about it. We all have it. Issues. With you it's low self-esteem triggered by loss of control. With me it's my mother. It's important that I learn to assert myself now when I feel that I'm being undermined. That's not a criticism, I'm just sharing my 'patterns' with you. I don't want to be a victim. My therapist is doing some good work with me and we're making a lot of progress. You should try it.

*Beat.*

Of course you only will when you're ready.

*Beat.*

Or desperate.

*LENNY laughs. MONA doesn't.*

I should have called.

MONA: I don't have a phone.

LENNY: Oh. Well at least you were in. I thought you might have been at church.

MONA: Church?

LENNY: Every Sunday.

MONA: But not today.

LENNY: Obviously.

MONA: Obviously.

*Pause.*

LENNY: Oh. Have you got plans? I hope I'm not –

MONA (*Matter of fact.*) No, no plans. Yes, you are interrupting. What do you want?

LENNY: Thought I'd drop by on the off chance.

MONA: Why did you come if you thought I'd be at church?

*Beat.*

LENNY: Here you are at home on a Sunday morning. In your dressing gown. What would your father say?

MONA: Luckily we'll never know. Well don't let me keep you.

LENNY: From what?

MONA: Anything. How about church?

LENNY: Church?

MONA: Yes.

LENNY: Depends on what you mean by church exactly.

MONA: The big house with the pointy bits on top. Lots of candles and dead people. Ring any bells?

LENNY: I express my faith in a different way now.

MONA: Me too. And I'll give you a clue. It involves dressing gowns. Anything else?

*Beat.*

LENNY: You don't go to church?

MONA: No.

LENNY: Not ever?

MONA: No, Lenny. Never.

LENNY: And you say I'm the one that's changed?

MONA: Why you making such a big deal about it?

LENNY: Because I remember your father. Your belief in God was unquestionable. Your father made sure of that. I'm amazed you've joined the legions of non-believers.

MONA: Who says I don't believe?

LENNY: I thought –

*Pause.*

MONA: You're still here.

LENNY: Yes.

*Beat.*

By the way I thought I might get you to read some of my book.

MONA: What's it called.

LENNY: It doesn't have a title. Yet.

MONA: Am I in it?

LENNY: Not exactly.

MONA: Couldn't I appear as a beautiful Nubian Queen? Cleopatra or something?

LENNY: It's *non*-fiction. A chronicle of my journey.

MONA: From where to where?

LENNY: From there to here.

*Beat.*

'From There To Here.' That's it. That's it! You see Mona? 'The Universe will provide.'

MONA: You think people will pay to listen to what you have to say?

LENNY: Pay? I don't know. What happens afterwards is out of my hands.

MONA: It's the journey, right?

LENNY: Right.

MONA: No-one's going to publish your book.

LENNY: They might.

MONA: They won't.

LENNY: How do you know?

MONA: I know all about publishing. See if I don't.

LENNY: Since when?

MONA: Since I worked in books.

LENNY: When did you work in books?

MONA: Six days a week for two years. Magnons. Don't you remember it?

LENNY: No.

MONA: Yes you do. That la-di-da bookshop in Highgate. The one that smelt of death. Susan probably knows it. I was amazed they gave me the job actually. I think the manager thought I looked good in the uniform.

LENNY: I'm sure you did.

MONA: I hated that manager. What was her name?

LENNY: I don't know.

MONA: You should. Miriam. All teeth and parma violets. I just kept my head down and did my work. Tried to keep the shop looking nice. I used to go through a can of furniture polish every day because it was the only thing that would mask that smell of death. Then here how this woman comes in dressed very nicely don't you know. Fox or something around she neck biting him own backside. She walking like she have a boiled sweet stuck up in her poom-poom. Ever so slowly she walking. And she going along the shelves like she Lady Muck. It might smell of death but at least I knew it was clean. And I know how to clean good and not pay somebody else to do it. Not like in Islington. Anyhow, there I am at the cash register and she walks up to the desk with her books, ready to pay. She looks around like there's been some kind of mistake. Then, in a voice that was so cut it could strip paint she says 'Excuse me. Do you speak English?'

LENNY: What did you say?

MONA: 'Yes, and I can read and write as well. Can I help you?' She never bat a eyelid. She just carry on like she sometin'. Well let me tell you, I'm sometin' too, Lenny. I'm somebody too! And don't you forget it!

*Pause.*

I shoulda lick her in her head. They might have fired me but it would have been worth it. I had nothing to lose, it's not as if I was ever going to get promoted. I suppose you could say my face didn't fit. Good enough to clean and serve, but not good enough for management. Not good enough to tell other people what to do. 'Can you speak English?' Yes. And I can skin a goat and cook a stew. I can mend a dress and I can dig a ditch. What can you do? I know what I know, and what I know is that they are not gonna publish a book by some two bit redskin drunk that nobody has ever heard of before. It's a business.

LENNY: I'm not interested in business.

MONA: Then your book gonna sit on the shelf for a very long time.

LENNY: So be it. All things for a reason. There's something else at work here, Mona. My Higher Power knows what's in store for me. And I trust Him. Her. Them.

MONA: Maybe He – She – It – They – want you to fail. Teach you a lesson.

LENNY: Failure is a choice. And I choose not to fail.

MONA: Really? You choose? Or does He – She – It – They – choose?

LENNY: The Higher Power doesn't want me to fail. I always believed that I was a failure. And I blamed everyone else for making me feel that I was. But actually I was perpetuating and inviting my own failures. It was easier than success. Success is really hard work. Failure is, relatively speaking –

MONA: Easy. Is all this in the book?

LENNY: Yes.

MONA: Riveting.

LENNY: Once I realised that I was essentially responsible for my failures and was subconsciously inviting them into my life, I also realised that I am powerless over it. So I decided to turn all the pain over to my Higher

Power and asked him with all the humility I could muster to cure me of this negativity. Now, you won't believe this but the most amazing thing happened. Since that day I have experienced success in areas of my life that I never thought possible. I just had to have the courage to ask. To offer it up to the Universe. It's much more powerful than I could or should ever be. My prayer was answered.

*Pause.*

MONA: So let me get this straight. Even though you don't seem to be able to remember much else, you do remember everyone around you making your life miserable and turning you into a failure. So one day you decided to ask your Higher Power, aka The Universe, to cure you and lo and behold you are now a runaway success?

LENNY: Your words. Not mine.

MONA: So which one of you is actually responsible for this…success you talking about?

LENNY: I can't be successful on my own. Anymore than we can live alone in the Universe. My Higher Power taught me that. But He – She – They –

MONA: Bloody hell, Lenny. Can't you just say 'God' or something?

LENNY: Why would that make it easier for you?

MONA: Frankly. Yes.

LENNY: Step Four. I made a decision to turn my will over to the care of God *as I understand him.*

MONA: Higher Power my arse.

*Beat.*

Or how about 'HP. The sauce of all knowledge?'

*MONA laughs. LENNY doesn't.*

LENNY: Have you noticed how you deflect when you are feeling uncomfortable?

MONA: Yes. That's what *normal* people do. It sends out the subtle but effective message 'You're pissing me off. Leave me alone.'

LENNY: What do you think would happen if you tried to go through that uncomfortable feeling? To experience it fully rather than reject it or make light of it.

MONA: I think I'd end up throwing boiling water in your face. I'm standing here in my dressing gown. I didn't get a wink of sleep last night. My head hurts and your aftershave is making my eyes water. So take a leaf out of your own book. Just take a deep breath and say whatever it is that you've got to say. 'Cos I know you didn't just 'drop by'.

*Pause.*

Why so nervous?

LENNY: Well, when dealing with a problem one has to be sure that one isn't merely solving one problem by replacing it with another. I read about a woman in Israel who swallowed a cockroach. Not on purpose. Obviously. No – it flew into her mouth. And lodged in her throat. She attempted to dislodge the cockroach with the end of a fork.

*Beat.*

She swallowed the fork.

MONA: Is that what you came here to tell me?

LENNY: No.

*Beat.*

Well…

*Pause.*

Can I have a glass of water?

*MONA fixes him with her stare.*

Right. OK. Part of the journey that I'm on requires me to take certain steps, as you know, as part of the recovery process.

MONA: Go on.

LENNY: Step Eight. I made –

MONA: No. No more book talk. Just me and you now.

LENNY: Making amends is part of that process. That's why I came back. I need to make amends with you.

*Pause.*

MONA: When you say 'need to' do you mean 'want to'?

LENNY: Yes. Of course.

MONA: And when you say 'make amends', do you actually mean 'ask forgiveness'?

LENNY: That's not the wording I would use necessarily.

MONA: I see. And what are you making amends for?

LENNY: For anything that I may, or may not, have done to you in the past.

MONA: And what do you think?

LENNY: I don't know.

MONA: Just give me a rough idea. Is it a couple of things, or should I put the kettle on and get comfortable?

LENNY: I don't know. Things that perhaps I did, unknowingly, that upset you?

MONA: Like?

LENNY: Well. We argued a lot. I know now that I wasn't fully aware or present in our relationship because of the drink. But I was powerless to do anything about it. I was a victim of my disease –

MONA: Disease?

LENNY: Yes, and that must have been hard for you. But I suffered too.

MONA: I can't believe I'm hearing this.

LENNY: I'm doing my best here. That's all I can do.

MONA: No, Lenny, you can try harder.

LENNY: Try? No I don't believe in trying. There is failure implicit in the word trying. I don't do trying. And I'm certainly not going to beg you to forgive me.

MONA: There! There it was.

LENNY: What?

MONA: I heard it. I nearly missed it under all the other rubbish, but I heard it. Finally, the F word. Forgiveness.

*A Pause. MONA continues gently –*

Why all this foolishness? Is it that difficult to say? Why didn't you just ask me?

LENNY: I don't know. I thought perhaps… I half expected you to still hold some kind of 'thing' against me.

MONA: Thing?

LENNY: Yes.

MONA: Like a grudge?

LENNY: Yes. Exactly.

MONA: You thought I would hold a grudge?

LENNY: Yes.

MONA: Against you?

*MONA laughs. LENNY joins in, relieved.*

LENNY: Yes. It was stupid of me really. Nerves got the better of me. But I can see now that you've obviously moved on.

MONA: Obviously.

*Pause.*

So did I used to be the kind of person who held grudges?

LENNY: Er… no but…but…

MONA: But-but – what?

LENNY: No. Well – I mean… No.

MONA: You see, I always thought grudges were what you held against someone if they had done you wrong.

LENNY: Yes.

MONA: So if I felt that someone had done me wrong, would it be wrong of me to hold something against that person? Say, a grudge?

LENNY: I couldn't say.

MONA: No. I suppose not.

*Pause.*

So?

LENNY: What?

MONA: Do you want me to forgive you or not?

LENNY: Yes. I suppose I do.

MONA: That wasn't so bad was it?

LENNY: No.

> *Pause.*
>
> Is that a yes?
>
> *MONA puts her hand to her forehead.*
>
> Mona?

MONA: I'm thinking.

LENNY: Look I can't force you. I've done what I can and I can do no more. All I can do is offer it up. The Universe will provide.

MONA: If that's the case, then why do you need me?

LENNY: Meaning?

MONA: Yes, Lenny. There is meaning in everything. You want something from me? Maybe I want something from you. Don't look so scared. Dinner. Tomorrow night. 8pm.

LENNY: Dinner?

MONA: I wonder if that place on Crawford street is still there?

LENNY: The Pepper Tree?

MONA: No, the place that Carlton had.

LENNY: The African?

MONA: Jamaican. The food there was always so good. And the seasoning… Carlton didn't know much. But he knew food. As we always said 'If it was good, a Jamaican did it. If it was bad?'

LENNY / MONA: 'A Jamaican did it.'

*They laugh. It is familiar, comfortable.*

LENNY: That place went out of business years ago. It's probably a Nando's by now. I'll find somewhere else. Somewhere special. Where we can talk. Deal?

MONA: Deal.

LENNY: Because we should talk, Mona.

MONA: Talk? OK.

*MONA goes to the mirror. She studies herself carefully.*

We did love each other once?

LENNY: Yes.

MONA: Thirty-two years and a faceful of wrinkles ago.

LENNY: Black don't crack.

MONA: Yes it does, Lenny. That's the problem.

*MONA's reflection becomes HETTIE. MONA stares transfixed.*

LENNY: Mona?

*Snap – MONA faces her own reflection. She is visibly shaken.*

Are you alright?

*MONA takes a deep breath, turns and faces LENNY, the picture of composure.*

MONA: A clear conscience for the price of a chicken dinner? I'd say that was a bargain.

# Scene Three

*MONA and LENNY stand facing each other. LENNY wears a suit and tie and is carrying flowers. MONA is wearing a revealing dress and has obviously been drinking.*

MONA: For me?

LENNY: A peace offering.

MONA: No need, Lenny. No need. Fancy seeing you here.

LENNY: 8pm on the dot.

MONA: I can't believe that I am the same size now as I was in High School. But look, a perfect fit. I found it hiding at the back of the cupboard. It's nothing special.

LENNY: You look fantastic.

MONA: Thank you. So do you. What's the occasion?

LENNY: Carlton's place is now a yoga centre so I booked a table at Carluccio's. 9pm.

MONA: How romantic. Is Susan with you? She doesn't have to sit in the car, Bring her in.

LENNY: No. She's having an evening out.

MONA: No Susan?

LENNY: No. You've got me all to yourself.

MONA: What do you mean?

LENNY: I'm confused. We had a date –

MONA: A date? Don't tell me I've –

*Beat.*

Oops.

LENNY: Oops.?

MONA: What a fool I am. There's been some kind of –
And here you are all dressed up.

LENNY: I came here so that we could talk. That was the
idea.

MONA: Talk? There's obviously been a misunderstanding.
I'm so sorry.

LENNY: No. There's no misunderstanding. You asked me to
come here. It was only last night for Christ's sake.

MONA: Did I say that?

LENNY: Yes.

MONA: Are you sure?

LENNY: I went straight out, booked a table and I've driven
halfway across London to come and pick you up. Of
course I'm sure.

MONA: I remember you saying you wanted to –

LENNY: Make amends –

MONA: Apologise – Yes, and I remember you asking me
out. But I don't remember making a firm arrangement.

LENNY: I didn't ask you out. You were the one who –

MONA: I don't remember –

LENNY: Don't be ridiculous –

MONA: Don't be angry. I'm really sorry, Lenny. I'd come
with you if I could.

*MONA slips on a pair of heels.*

You don't think it's too much?

LENNY: Depends.

MONA: On what?

LENNY: On where you're headed.

MONA: Bridge.

LENNY: Bridge?

MONA: Bridge. Yes.

LENNY: You never mentioned anything about bridge.

MONA: It's Monday.

LENNY: I know it's Monday.

MONA: Monday night is bridge night.

LENNY: But you never go out.

MONA: So what's all this? Scotch mist?

*MONA smoothes her skirt and adjusts her stockings.*

You really don't think this is too much? You would say wouldn't you? Does it make my behind look big?

*LENNY looks.*

LENNY: Huge.

MONA: Good. You might have developed a taste for flat-bottom white women, but it's good to see that you can still appreciate the fuller figure. The bridge set always dress nice. We might be a little older, but we're still attractive. I might not win Miss Jamaica but I can still mix it better than Sylvia Harvey. Anybody can mix it better than Sylvia Harvey.

LENNY: This is unbelievable. Right. I'll give you a lift. We can talk on the way.

*MONA hesitates. She goes to the mirror and fixes her earrings. She catches her reflection –*

Mona?

*A peal of laughter, off.*

Mona?

MONA: What?

LENNY: Where are you going?

MONA: It's out of your way.

LENNY: I don't mind.

MONA: I do. If you hurry you could go to the restaurant with Susan. She probably need fattening up. You know how these white women do.

LENNY: I told you. She's out. With friends.

MONA: Yes. Important for her to spend time with people her own age.

LENNY: I knew this was a mistake. That's it. I'm going home.

MONA: Wait.

LENNY: What?

MONA: Let me make it up to you.

LENNY: Aren't you going to be late?

MONA: What for?

LENNY: Bridge.

*MONA begins to sway to the music.*

Look. I think we should talk about – about what I mentioned yesterday. I want to be able to move on. We both should.

MONA: Hmm?

LENNY: Step Eight. Made a list of all persons we had harmed, and became willing to make amends to them all.

MONA: Uh-huh.

LENNY: Step Nine. Made direct amends to such people wherever possible, except when to do so would injure them or others.

*MONA stretches out a hand towards LENNY.*

MONA: For old times' sake.

LENNY: I thought we were talking.

MONA: You were talking. Come.

LENNY: Why?

MONA: Give. Stop asking questions.

LENNY: You gonna read my palm?

MONA: I don't need your palm to read you, Lenny.

*LENNY extends his hand.*

The steps I know are much more interesting than yours. Jive? Swing? Two Step?

LENNY: Here?

MONA: Why not?

LENNIE: There isn't enough –

MONA: We'll make room.

LENNY: This isn't a good idea.

MONA: You really know how to make a girl go off the boil.

*MONA begins to move the furniture to one side, clearing a space in which they can move. LENNY watches –*

I've just noticed your suit. Very nice. I like a man who's well turned out. There was a time when a man wouldn't have been seen dead without a tie and hat. Is it too much to ask? A tie and a hat? These days I think I'd be happy to see a man in a pair of trousers that fitted him properly.

*MONA surveys her 'dance area' clearly pleased with herself.*

Right. Make yourself useful. Cupboard behind you. Right side draw. Top shelf. You see it?

LENNY: What am I looking for?

MONA: Jim Beam, Cutty Sark or Jamesons. Help yourself.

LENNY: You know I don't.

MONA: Please yourself. Me? I think I dance better with a little something inside me.

*Beat.*

So – Are you going to fix me a drink?

LENNY: There's no ice.

MONA: I'll just take a little water.

LENNY: Fine.

*LENNY stares at the whiskey bottle.*

MONA: What's the matter?

LENNY: Nothing.

MONA: Good. I'll have a Jamesons. And whatever you're having.

*MONA stands watching LENNY as he takes out a tumbler and the bottle of whiskey. He pours a steady measure.*

Just a little water. To improve the flavour. Isn't that what you used to say?

LENNY: Did I? I don't remember.

*He passes the glass to MONA who drains it in one gulp.*

MONA: I know you like a woman who knows how to dance.

LENNY: I like a woman who knows when to stop.

MONA: Well I could keep going all night. This brings back memories. The music. The dancing. Sorry I forgot you don't remember anything do you?

LENNY: I remember dancing. Of course I do.

MONA: Good. I'll have another.

*She holds out her glass. LENNIE takes it and pours her another drink. His movements are measured, controlled.*

LENNY: Enough?

MONA: Plenty.

(*As LENNY.*) 'Some men might want to take advantage you know. I've seen it happen. So it wouldn't surprise me if some women thought that some men were out to juice them a little. And some women would be right about some men. Some of the time that's true. But not always.'

LENNY: I said that?

*Handing her the glass.*

Here.

MONA: Thank you.

*Pause.*

You come here often?

LENNY: (*As MONA.*) Every Thursday with my sister.

*They laugh. Recognition.*

MONA: (*As LENNY.*) You look nice.

LENNY: (*As MONA.*) Thank you. I'd say the same but it's too dark in here to tell.

MONA: (*As LENNY.*) I wondered why you were squinting.

LENNY: (*As MONA.*) I'm looking for your good points.

MONA: (*As LENNY.*) Then I suggest you look lower.

*LENNY has been outfoxed. He can't remember what came next.*

LENNY: I said that?

MONA: Yes.

LENNY: I'm surprised you didn't slap me.

MONA: I was giving you the benefit of the doubt.

LENNY: Then you complimented me on my double chin.

MONA: (*As LENNY.*) You know how much chicken I have to eat to keep a chin like this?

LENNY: (*As MONA.*) You're growing it?

MONA: (*As LENNY.*) My mother always said 'Never trust a man with a small chin'.

LENNY: My mother always said 'Never trust a man'.

*The dancing becomes more fluid. They are good. Suddenly LENNY steps on MONA's foot.*

MONA: Ow!

*She hands him her glass and grabs her foot.*

LENNY: Did you stand on my foot or did I stand on yours?

MONA: I stood on yours I think.

LENNY: Yes. The heels. I remember.

MONA: You said 'You have delicate feet. I didn't feel a thing.'

LENNY: (*As MONA.*) That's a very gentlemanly thing to say.

MONA: (*As LENNY.*) Looks like I'll have to keep my eye on you.

LENNY: (*As MONA.*) Don't look too close you might see the join.

MONA: (*As LENNY.*) Drink up and I'll teach you the Rumba.

*LENNY tosses back the drink in one gulp. He freezes.*

I'm sure you'll pick it up very quickly. Just watch me. Like this.

LENNY: Bitch.

MONA: (*As LENNY.*) It's all in the hips.

LENNY: Bitch.

MONA: (*As LENNY.*) Don't you want to? Maybe you could come back to my place for a nightcap instead?

LENNY: You cruel bitch. Why would you do that?

MONA: Because I know you're in there somewhere.

LENNY: Why do you hate me so much?

MONA: Oh. Now let me see. Is it because you were the first man that I slept with? Is it because I only did it because you said we were gonna get married? Is it because you ran to Gloria?

LENNY: You made me take a drink!

MONA: I didn't touch you. Always someone else's fault.

LENNY: Oh God – I need –

MONA: Your needs aren't important to me.

LENNY: OK. Let's just think this through – talk this through –

MONA: Stop being so reasonable.

LENNY: But it's the only way to –

MONA: I hate fucking reasonable.

LENNY: But I don't want –

MONA: I don't care what you want! You don't get to choose this time round. Why am I even talking to you? I don't know you. Get out of my way. Yes, you! Step aside you sap. You shadow. At least my Lenny had guts. At least my Lenny had balls. At least my Lenny was alive!

LENNY: That's not true. I suffered –

MONA: Show me!

MONA: I lost a child!

LENNY: I-know-I-know-I-know-I-know-I-know! But you can't keep playing that card. I know it was painful, difficult. But these things happen. It wasn't a child it was –

MONA: Don't you dare –

LENNY: Blood. There was blood – But she wasn't –

MONA: She?

LENNY: What?

MONA: You said she.

LENNY: She. He. It wasn't –

MONA: She was.

LENNY: But she was never –

MONA: Alive? If I can see you, are you alive? If I can smell you, are you alive? If I can hear you, are you alive?

*LENNY goes to the door: it is locked.*

LENNY: You have no right to punish me like this.

MONA: Answer the question.

LENNY: Jesus Christ, you made me drink, Mona. That has very serious repercussions. You have to let me go.

MONA: Why should I?

LENNY: (*Shouting.*) Because none of this is my fault!

*Pause.*

You had a miscarriage and for that I am truly, truly sorry. But that was thirty-two years ago. I'm sorry that we didn't stay together. I'm sorry that I got so drunk that night because I couldn't…cope. I'm sorry I ran to Gloria. And I'm sorry that I didn't come back. I'm sorry that you've been alone all these years. I'm sorry that you never had a child of your own. I'm sure that I'm mixed up in there somewhere along the road, and I'll take that on the chin. But, you had a miscarriage, Mona. A miscarriage. I'm not to blame for that.

*Pause.*

MONA: Is that so?

*Pause.*

You haven't suffered, Lenny. And if you did, it's long forgotten. She's with me all the time.

*MONA looks around the room frantically. She calls to HETTIE.*

Tell him. Tell him how you follow me everywhere I go. I can't go to the Supermarket anymore, I can't even go to church because I know that God is looking down on me. Punishing me. Judging me. For what we did. For what you did. Tell him –

LENNY: You still feel guilty? After all these years your father's voice still ringing in your ears? Is that what this is about? We didn't do anything wrong –

MONA: Of course it was wrong. We weren't even married.

LENNY: You did it because you liked it.

MONA: I did it because you wanted me. All the time you wanted me. Any chance to do it –

LENNY: We were young. And passionate –

MONA: No –

LENNY: Let's face it. We were good at it –

MONA: No.

LENNY: We enjoyed it.

MONA: I never enjoyed it. It was wrong. You were the one who wanted it –

LENNY: I didn't force you.

MONA: Yes you did!

*Pause.*

Drink has many, many uses. A little nip can relax you. A couple of glasses can loosen your tongue. Drink enough and it will loosen your resolve. And let's face it, Lenny, drink makes you horny.

LENNY: What?

MONA: Persistent.

LENNY: Mona.

MONA: And strong.

LENNY: You make it sound as though –

MONA: What?

*Beat.*

LENNY: It's not my fault.

MONA: I lost a child. Whose fault was it?

LENNY: I don't know. But that's not how it – I don't remember, but I –

MONA: I tried to stop you. But it was too late.

LENNY: You said you loved me. I thought you wanted to.

MONA: My father didn't drag me to church week in week out and me not learn anything. You forced me. There was blood. I tried to stop you but you were –

LENNY: Oh, God.

MONA: Insistent.

LENNY: I just don't remember.

MONA: How convenient.

LENNY: But I'd been drinking. So I wasn't to blame. It was… I didn't… I'm… I'm… I was powerless to… It's not. It's not…

MONA: Come on, Lenny.

LENNIE: I don't remember!

MONA: I know you're in there.

LENNY: Oh God – Oh God – Oh God –

*LENNY pulls frantically on the door handle.*

I have to go.

MONA: So go.

LENNY: I can't.

MONA: Then stay.

LENNY: I can't! The door is locked.

MONA: Oh.

LENNY: Open it.

MONA: Not quite sure where I put the keys.

LENNY: Mona.

MONA: So forgetful. Just like you.

LENNY: You said that you could forgive and forget.

MONA: Who said anything about forgiving?

LENNY: You did.

MONA: No. You did. You asked me to forgive you.

LENNY: Yes. I thought –

MONA: You thought wrong!

LENNY: Open the door. Jesus Christ, Mona, this is serious. Open the door.

MONA: Why are you in such a hurry?

LENNY: At least let me use the phone.

MONA: Susan waiting up for you?

LENNY: I have to call someone.

MONA: Who?

*LENNY is frantic, disorientated.*

LENNY: I need… I just need…

MONA: A drink? Good idea. Fix me one too while you're at it.

LENNY: GIVE ME THE PHONE!

MONA: I don't have a phone.

*LENNY is frozen with panic.*

Now. Fix me a drink.

LENNY: Let me out. Now. You have to let me out or I swear to God I'll –

MONA: Just a small one.

LENNY: Bitch.

MONA: Actually, make that a large.

LENNY: Bitch.

MONA: And whatever you're having.

*LENNY's anger and hatred spills over uncontrollably.*

LENNY: BITCH FUCKING BITCH FUCKING BITCH YOU BITCH FUCKING BITCH

MONA: (*As if to HETTIE.*) Are you watching this? Now do you see?

*LENNY throws the bottle of whiskey, smashing it –*

LENNY: FUCK YOU, YOU FUCKING BITCH!

*MONA moves towards him –*

MONA: Yes. Yes.

LENNY: I'LL FUCKING KILL YOU, BITCH!

*He lunges at her and immediately checks himself in horror. MONA is triumphant.*

MONA: Welcome home, Lenny.

# Scene Four

*AJ and MONA stand facing each other. Silence.*

AJ: Where is he?

*Pause.*

The question ain't difficult. Read my lips or turn up your hearing aid, one or the other. Where. Is. He?

*Pause.*

MONA: I. Don't. Know.

AJ: So why did you let me in?

MONA: I wanted to see if –

*Beat.*

I wanted to see if you were as handsome as your father. You look –

AJ: Like him? Yeah, yeah, whatever. I need to talk to him.

MONA: Sounds urgent.

AJ: Just tell me, yeah, so I can get the fuck outta here.

MONA: Seeing as you asked so nicely.

*Pause.*

What's AJ short for?

AJ: Aled fucking Jones all it matters to you.

MONA: It's probably Anthony something. You look like an Anthony.

AJ: Nobody calls me that.

MONA: Bingo. Case closed.

AJ: No shit, Sherlock. Every black family has a Tony in there somewhere. You ain't so clever.

MONA: Neither are you if you can't find your own father.

*Pause.*

What makes you think I know where he is?

AJ: He's always round here lately. Doing his 'ting'.

MONA: He told you?

AJ: He don't tell me shit. Mum told me.

MONA: Really? Susan knows?

AJ: We both know. I know he was here last night.

MONA: He wanted to talk.

AJ: Yeah, yeah. Step Nine. Did he do it?

MONA: He said he wanted to –

AJ: Make amends. I know, I live with this shit all the time. How did it go?

MONA: You interested?

AJ: No. Just making polite conversation.

MONA: So sarcastic.

AJ: So sue me.

MONA: I told him that he has ruined my life. I told him that he could take his apology and shove it up his sorry black arse.

*Pause.*

You seem –

AJ: What?

MONA: Anxious.

AJ: If my dad comes by, tell him to call home.

MONA: Is something wrong?

AJ: Should it be?

MONA: You just seem… I don't know, it just seems strange. You and Susan seem to know so much about this situation and yet you don't know how it went last night?

AJ: Like I said we don't talk much.

MONA: Were you out last night?

AJ: Look at me. You don't think I keep this locked up in the house 24/7 do you?

MONA: Like father like son. When I was your age –

AJ: When you were my age, the animals were still coming in two by two! Now, I ain't got time for this. If you can't help. I'm outta here.

MONA: Now I see. He didn't come home last night.

*Beat.*

AJ: Says who?

MONA: Did he?

AJ: I ain't his keeper.

MONA: You think I was the last person to see him… Alive, I was going to say. How silly is that? Even so, I can see why you came. I'd be worried too.

AJ: Who says I'm worried?

MONA: You're here aren't you?

*Beat.*

And you think –

AJ: I don't think anything. I just wanna find him.

MONA: In case he's gone and done something silly?

AJ: You're confusing me with someone who gives a shit.

MONA: So why did you come.

AJ: When I got my mum burning up my Nokia all night, stressing me out, wanting to know where my dad is, then I start to get vex.

MONA: Must have been hard on you growing up with all that –

AJ: If you can't help me –

MONA: AJ –

AJ: Don't chat my name like you know me. But then maybe you do? Bet dad's been round here blabbin' all our business.

MONA: But he still cares.

AJ: No he don't. He ain't in the house long enough to care. Too busy at college. Too busy writing. Too busy with people like you –

*AJ notices the flowers in the vase.*

Bet these are from him.

MONA: A peace offering.

AJ: Thass what I mean. He don't do that shit for me. Every birthday. Year in year out. No card. No present. No-thing. It got so bad that last year my mum *made* him go out and get me something. What did he get me? Mittens. Not gloves. Mittens.

MONA: Oh. Were they… nice mittens?

AJ: Who cares? My birthday is in July!

MONA: Ah.

AJ: Damn right fuckin' 'ah'. But you know what, thass fine by me. If he wants to go off and commune with his inner child then so be it. Just don't expect me to come along for the ride.

MONA: That does sound hard.

AJ: Fuck off.

MONA: I'm on your side.

AJ: No you ain't! You're the one getting the fuckin' apology! Every day he comes round here is another day he ain't at home. Every day he's making things up to you, he ain't at home making things up with us. He came round here last night to make amends? Well lucky fucking you. The rest of us are still waiting in line.

MONA: I'm sorry.

AJ: Is it?

*AJ sneezes.*

Fucking rain. Black people and water don't mix.

*Beat.*

I always used to tell that to my teachers, but they wouldn't listen. I was just a kid what did I know? Every week I'd say 'Black people don't like water' and every week they'd still drag me down that fucking Lido.

*Beat.*

How fucked up is that?

*Beat.*

They used to take us to this dirty old place down Tooting. I couldn't stand it. Only crazy ass teachers would make school-kids swim around in some other school-kids' piss. I begged my dad to let me have a sick-note so I wouldn't have to go swimming in all that nastiness. But instead of taking my side, hear how he goes. 'The reason you don't like swimming is because you don't know *how* to swim. So I'm going to teach you.' This was a new one on me, 'cos we never did shit together.

So there I am at Tooting Bec Lido sitting on the side, looking down into the yellow water. And Dad's in there, swimming around, going underwater, letting the piss go in his mouth and everything. 'Don't be such a pussy.' He goes. 'Get in.' It was like I was stuck to the ground. I just couldn't do it. Not because of the yellow water, but because I knew that I would sink like a fuckin' brick. Dad's telling me how if I was in the Dead Sea, the salt would hold me up and shit. I'm thinking 'I don't care how much salt you put in there, I'm still gonna fuckin' sink and anyhow I ain't in the Dead Sea. I'm in Totting Bec Pissing Lido!'

See how my feet are dangling in the water 'cos I'm trying to show willing, yeah, but all the time thinking 'No way. No fucking way.' Dad is calling out to me and by now people are looking over, what with him having a loud mouth and all. Especially after a couple of drinks. 'Come in. Don't be scared. I'll catch you.' I'll admit it. I was scared. I thought to myself 'You best do it now dread before people start looking for real.' I look down at him, at this long black shadow in the water, sleek as a fuckin' shark. 'It's alright. I'm here. I'll catch you.' He's got his arms out, ready, so I take a deep breath and I just fling myself into the water towards him. The last thing I saw before I hit the water was my Dad backing away from me, pulling his arms out of my reach.

The shock hit me just like the water hit me. Hard. I don't know how much I swallowed. Thrashing around trying to reach out and grab hold of something, anything. No matter what I did I felt my body sinking like a stone. I didn't even know which way was up and all I could taste was piss, chlorine and rain.

Somehow I struggled to the side of the pool. No-one helped me you know. See me there, clinging to the side, gasping for breath. I was still shaking, snot coming out my nose, my eyes red. I look around and everybody – and I mean *everybody* – is staring at me. And there standing over me at the poolside was my Dad.

'Best way to learn,' he goes. 'Sink or swim.'

I scrambled out of the pool, trying not to catch anybody's eye. But I knew they was all still watching. As I went to get changed I could feel the shame hanging off me like a wet towel, dread.

*Beat.*

We didn't speak until we got to the car, and all he said was…

*Beat.*

'Macdonalds?'

*Pause.*

MONA: We have more in common than you think. I was a disappointment to my father too.

AJ: Who you calling a disappointment?

MONA: Wait. That's not –

AJ: Who?

MONA: That's not how I meant it –

AJ: You fucking bitch. Who the fuck are you to call me a disappointment.?

MONA: I know it's hard. I see the kids round here. Not many opportunities for the youth. And it's bad enough for the black kids, let alone the half-caste ones.

AJ: Who you callin' half-caste? I know you on your last legs and all, but what kind of old fashioned shit is that?

MONA: Don't raise your voice to me.

AJ: I'm Bi-racial. It ain't hard. You should know better than that, black as you are.

MONA: You don't know who you are any more than your father does.

AJ: Stop chattin' my business!

MONA: Don't shout at me.

AJ: Or what?

MONA: Don't you threaten me.

AJ: You don't know shit. I'm going. Stench in her mek me feel sick anyhow. Try using a window.

MONA: Try using the door!

AJ: You know what? My Dad was right about you. You're a fucking charity case. He only comes round here 'cos he feels sorry for you. Jesus I've heard of lonely but you really are fucked.

MONA: You know…your bad language really sets my teeth on edge.

AJ: Tek 'em out then!

MONA: I thought you were different. You don't know it yet, but I'm much better at this than you are. You too soft. Your heart's too warm. I was prepared to give you the benefit of the doubt. But you are just like your father.

*A noise from offstage.*

From now on picknie – You're on your own.

*LENNY enters. He is barefoot and his hair is nappy. He looks terrible. He clocks AJ and is rooted to the spot.*

There's coffee in the pot. I make sure I *grind* it just the way you like it.

*Pause.*

Just a little sugar, right Lenny?

AJ: So whass going on?

*Pause.*

Don't I even get a hello? I've had pure drama off Mum 'cos a you. That ain't nothin'. Why didn't you come home last night?

MONA: It was late.

AJ: You could have called.

LENNY: I need my socks and I need my shoes.

MONA: And?

LENNY: Where are they?

MONA: Try under the bed.

*Pause.*

AJ: Under the bed? Under the fuckin' – nah nah nah I ain't even going there. You mean to tell me that while I been up all night listening to mum crying her eyes out, wondering what the hell has happened to you… all the time you was here, grinding up this old bag o' bones?

MONA: Who you callin' old?

AJ: Don't worry, I'll be dealing with you later. Right now it's you, Dad. Thass what I'm interested in.

*Pause.*

What? Why you ain't sayin' nothin'?

*Pause.*

Well – you got balls, I'll give you that. Thought they dried up a long time ago, dread. Enjoy it while you can, grandma, 'cos you gonna be dead soon anyhow. Oh, and when you're laying on your back with your legs in the air? Just remember, he don't care about you.

MONA: The fact that your father was willing to make amends to me, well, that shows how much he cares, doesn't it?

AJ: Don't flatter yourself. You ain't the first.

MONA: Neither were you. You're still in line.

AJ: Fuck you!

MONA: Are you gonna let him speak to me like that, Lenny? You should show some respect.

AJ: Respect you? You're just plain nasty. I seen videos with old women like you and always wondered where they find 'em. Now I know.

LENNY: That's enough –

AJ: Nah – you don't get to come over all Dad on me now. Not after this. I come 'cos mum asked me to. She was scared. Really scared.

*Beat.*

Are you coming home?

*Pause.*

Dad. Are you coming home?

*Pause.*

Well?

*LENNY makes to leave.*

MONA: (*With as much bravura as she can muster.*) Leaving so soon? Well – I can't tell you how nice it was to spend quality time with you last night, Lenny.

LENNY (*Steely.*) And I can't tell you either.

AJ: Talk to *me.* You ain't got no business with her.

MONA: Look, I don't want to pick a fight with you.

AJ: Shoulda thought of that before you start grinding my Dad. Standing there doin' nothin'? Wass the matter with you?

MONA: It's not his fault.

AJ: Then who?

MONA: If you'd just listen for a second –

AJ: Listen to your lies? Listen to a dried up bitch like you?

LENNY: AJ!

MONA: Truce! Alright? Truce.

*Beat.*

It's my fault, AJ.

*Beat.*

This is all getting out of hand. I have to try…and explain. We were just old friends having dinner, alright? But as I said, the evening just got a little –

AJ: What?

MONA: A little out of hand. Isn't that right, Lenny? We had a meal. We danced.

*Beat.*

But after a couple of drinks it seemed best for your father to stay here. Just to be on the safe side. So then –

AJ: Wait –

MONA: What?

AJ: He don't drink. So now I know you lying.

LENNY: That's enough.

MONA: I know he doesn't which is why I was so surprised when –

LENNY: Mona!

MONA: But we shouldn't dwell on the past. After all – 'We can't change yesterday. Tomorrow is still unknown. Only today.'

AJ: Dad? Did you have a drink?

MONA: Don't judge him. It's not right. Only God can do that.

AJ: Did you?

*Beat.*

I ain't messin' with you.

LENNY: Not ain't –

AJ: Fuck you. Answer the question.

*LENNY raises his hand involuntarily.*

MONA: Lenny! Remember the Steps. First, acknowledge the problem. Secondly, acknowledge that the problem is probably not your fault.

*Silence.*

AJ: Dad. I'm sorry. Let's just get out of here, yeah? Get you home.

*Beat.*

Say something.

*Beat.*

What is it with you?

*Beat.*

Dad?

*Beat.*

So what, we just gonna go on pretending that everything's fine?

*Beat.*

Why can't you talk to me? Nothing bad's gonna happen.

*Pause.*

LENNY: Wait in the car. We'll talk about this later.

AJ: Dad!

LENNY: (*Firmly.*) Not. Now. I have to be the man that I am. Not the man that you want me to be. I'm sorry.

*LENNY reaches out his hand to AJ. He pulls away.*

AJ: Don't pat me on the head, you fuck.
That ain't what I was asking you to do.

Do I look like a fucking dog to you?
Fuck you.
Fuck you.

*LENNY exits slowly towards the bedroom. Silence. AJ presses his fingers into his eyes desperate to hold back the tears. MONA involuntarily moves towards him to comfort him, but checks herself. LENNY enters with his socks and shoes.*

LENNY: You have anything to say?

MONA: No. I think we're done.

LENNY *(To AJ.)* I'll be in the car.

*LENNY pulls on his jacket and moves to the front door. He stretches out his hand to the door handle, remembers that it will be locked. Turns to look at MONA.*

MONA: It's open.

*LENNY, mistrustful to the last pauses before trying the door. It opens. He exits without looking back. After a moment –*

I didn't mean to…

*Pause.*

Big man like you? You'll be OK.

*Pause.*

It's not my fault! You just got caught up, that's all.

*The sound of a car engine. AJ moves quickly to the door but he is too late. The sound of the car fades into the distance.*

*(Barely audible.)* Damn you, Lenny.

*As AJ fishes in his pocket for a cigarette, HETTIE enters behind MONA. AJ searches his pockets for a light. HETTIE points to a box of matches on the sideboard. AJ sees them, lights the cigarette and inhales as if composing himself. When he is ready he turns and makes for the door.*

I meant what I said earlier. You do look just like him.

AJ: It could be worse. I could look like you.

HETTIE: Me?

*MONA spins around.*

MONA: Leave me alone!

AJ: Who you talkin' to?

MONA: No-one.

AJ: You crazy-ass bitch.

MONA: I'm not crazy. I'm… I'm…

AJ: Try sorry.

MONA: Sorry? No. Yes. I feel…

AJ: You know what? Save it. You feel bad now, yeah? But when you're on your deathbed? When you're gasping for your last breath? And there ain't nobody there with you? It's gonna feel much, much worse.

## Scene Five

*The following week. The flat is a mess. There are food cartons, items of clothing, broken crockery etc littering the floor. HETTIE sits at the table eating a sandwich. She devours it hungrily, washing it down with a mug of tea. MONA enters full of purpose. She has a large bag into which she is packing items of clothing.*

HETTIE: Can't sleep?

MONA: Piss off!

*MONA stuffs a few items of clothing into the bag. Grabbing at things as she goes.*

HETTIE: Anger kicks
As conscience pricks…

*MONA ignores her and continues. HETTIE begins to giggle.*

MONA: What?

HETTIE: You can't leave.

MONA: Watch me.

*HETTIE puts down her sandwich and tea and watches her.*

What?

*HETTIE continues to stare.*

When I'm gone? Then you'll be sorry.

*MONA zips up her bag.*

I'm leaving.

*MONA faces the front door, unable to move.*

HETTIE: Tip and sway
Ebb and flow
Hearts laid low
Like ulcers grow.

MONA: I'm stronger than you think.

*MONA walks slowly to the door. Very deliberately she turns each key and releases the lock. She pauses. Her hand reaches out to the door handle. A moment's hesitation – her hand drops to her side, defeated.*

Damn you.

*HETTIE begins to giggle, her laughter increasing.*

HETTIE: You see? I know you never could.
So now I know I stay for good.

MONA: Bitch!

*MONA throws herself at the door, grabs the handle and flings it wide. LENNY stands there framed in the doorway. He looks terrible. He fixes his gaze on MONA and steps purposefully in.*

LENNY: Well – this is the bit that you've been waiting for. 'Bring out the drunk! All rise for the drunk!' People love a good drunk.

*MONA takes a step towards the door. LENNY is too quick for her. He closes the door, locks it.*

Best not leave the door open, Mona. It's not safe.

*Silence.*

I didn't know where else to go.

*Pause.*

Let me fix you a drink.

*LENNY goes to the cupboard –*

Right side draw. Top shelf. Ah-a! Jim Beam, Cutty Sark or Jamesons?

*MONA doesn't answer. He pours two Jamesons and adds water.*

Just a little water. To improve the flavour.

*LENNY places one of the glasses on the table in front of MONA.*

You know what I love about drinking? It's the familiarity. I know where I am when I have a drink. Wherever you are in the world, when you have a drink, you're home.

*Pause.*

Haven't you forgotten something?

MONA: Cheers.

LENNY: It's Monday.

*Beat.*

Bridge.

MONA: Bridge?

LENNY: Bridge. Yes. I'd offer you a lift but…

*Beat.*

You're not going dressed like that are you? Mind you I can't talk. I look like shit too.

*MONA tries to exit to the kitchen. HETTIE blocks her way.*

Are you alright? You seem –

MONA: What?

LENNY: Anxious.

*Beat.*

No need. None of this is your fault. And the other night? Well – I was frustrated that I couldn't remember. And the shock when I realized…

Thanks to you, I realise what kind of man I was and how difficult it must have been for you. I was insatiable. That was my problem. I always wanted it and you were too naïve to know how to stop me. You know how it is. I'm a man. And consequently flawed.

Sexual appetite is one thing, but what I did to you… Forcing you to…

It's important that you understand how terrible I feel about what I did to you. I came because I thought you should see me like this. I thought it might… Help.

I'm so ashamed.

Ashamed, alone and on the M25. Like a homing pigeon. Here I am, a grown man, and I end up back at my mother's. That really was the final humiliation.

I told her what had happened, just as you told me. I told her everything.

HETTIE: (*To MONA.*) Everything?

LENNY: Everything. And talking about those things with my mother. That was difficult. She doesn't really understand. 'Lenny,' she says, 'you can't have a miscarriage through having sex.'

*Beat.*

That thought never crossed my mind. Of course you and I both know different. I tried to explain to her, that it must have been me, what I did. Forcing you to –

She sends her regards to you by the way.

*LENNY rummages in his pockets.*

I slept in my old room. You won't believe the things I found. Look at this… That bus ticket might be worth a fortune now. Concert tickets…

*He takes out a photograph.*

That's you and me outside the 100 Club with…

*LENNY takes out a pack of cigarettes.*

Pack of Peter Stuyvesant. God does anyone still smoke those things? Oh – and I found this.

*LENNY takes out a letter.*

MONA: Don't move.
Don't breathe…

*Beat.*

HETTIE: He knows.

MONA: No. Just –

LENNY: Ring any bells?

MONA: Yes. No.

LENNY: Are you alright? You seem –

MONA: Confused? Yes. I am a little –

LENNY: Allow me to clarify.

> *LENNY begins to read the letter.*

> 'You have captured the very essence of me.
> I want to give myself to you entirely – '

> *LENNY hands the letter to MONA.*

> I didn't realise you had such a rich vocabulary.

> *MONA reads the letter.*

HETTIE: Your touch is all I think about
Your kisses turn me inside out

MONA: No. That's not… I was –

LENNY: Naïve? This letter says otherwise.

HETTIE: The heat of your blood warms my soul
Our bodies merge –

MONA: That's not me.

LENNY: Not naïve?

HETTIE: Not likely.

MONA: (*To HETTIE.*) Stop it!

LENNY: Stop? Is that what you said to me? Stop Lenny?

MONA: I told you what happened.

LENNY: Remind me again.

MONA: I know what happened. I was there.

HETTIE: I was there. A glint in your eye.
  She wanted you.

LENNY: You wanted me.

MONA: No. It was wrong. We shouldn't have.

LENNY: But we did. And you wanted to. We wanted to.

MONA: You. You –

LENNY: Made me?

HETTIE: You made me whole.

MONA: Shut up.

HETTIE: Made me complete.

*MONA tears up the letter.*

  Tell him how you nursed me
  Fed me on the crusts of your hatred
  Til my hair curled, unfurled
  Across your lonely pillow.

LENNY: You lied.

HETTIE: All because you wanted him.

MONA: Says who?

LENNY: You lied! You wanted it as much as I did.

MONA: Alright! I lied – I lied – I lied – I lied – I lied!

*Beat.*

  It doesn't matter. By the time you've sobered up, you
  won't even remember.

LENNY: Me? Oh, I'm as sober as a judge.

*Beat.*

I wanted to be fully aware and present for this moment.

MONA: I don't believe you. Look at you –

LENNY: Looks can be deceiving. Can't they, Mona?

MONA: 'Bring out the drunk. Everybody loves a drunk.' You told me.

LENNY: I'm a drunk alright. I know exactly what I am. I just choose not to drink anymore.

*LENNY pours his glass of whiskey onto the floor.*

I'm still living in the bottle, Mona. There's just no alcohol in it.

*Beat.*

I bet you pictured me in a seedy bar somewhere, drowning my sorrows. Knocking back the whiskey. Sorry to disappoint.

*Beat.*

I should have listened to my mother. 'Lenny?' she says, 'I have nothing against Mona, but that girl easy like Sunday morning.'

*LENNY begins to collect up his things.*

Well. I think we're all done here. Unless…?

MONA: No. We're done.

*LENNY turns and makes his way to the door.*

HETTIE: We could…

MONA: I can't.

HETTIE: We should…

MONA: Leave me alone!

HETTIE: It's your fault Hettie stays you know
You should have fucking let me go!

MONA: Get out get out get out get –

HETTIE: Shout. Shout.
Get out get out –

MONA: (*To LENNY.*) Tell her! Tell her to…

LENNY: Tell who?

*Pause.*

Mona?

*Pause.*

Are you – ?

MONA: Alright?

*Pause.*

(*To HETTIE.*) I don't know how.

HETTIE: (*As MONA.*) 'Something in blue, or then perhaps
A simple cotton dress with straps.'

MONA: How do you know?

HETTIE: I was there. A glint in your eye.

MONA: You were there?

HETTIE: Beside you. Inside you.

MONA: (*To LENNY.*) What was I wearing?

LENNY: When?

MONA: Then.

HETTIE: A simple cotton dress…

MONA: With straps?

HETTIE: Yes.

MONA: Yes. Pulled over my head, my arms raised, I felt –

MONA / HETTIE: Vulnerable.

MONA: Soft. For the first time. I knew that my secret was
beginning to show itself. And as the dress slipped over
my body it felt –

*Beat.*

Good.

HETTIE: (*Encouragingly.*) Good.

MONA: The sweat was beading on my skin. My heart was
racing. My mouth was dry. I flooded at the thought of
you… 'Soon come, Lenny. Soon come.'

HETTIE: You checked the mirror, just to see
Then out the door and on the 73.

MONA: The bus was full, I remember that. And there was
nowhere to sit. Nobody got up for me.

HETTIE: Your belly tight
But not quite showing
Yet all the time growing

MONA: They weren't to know, I suppose.

HETTIE:
The bus swung around like a big black woman dancing
Grindin' and windin' by the light of the moon
Jiggling an wriggling to a Miles Davis tune
That none of us could hear but the driver and the bus –

MONA: You.

HETTIE: Me.

MONA / HETTIE: Us.

HETTIE: Finally
    Easily
    The ecstasy subsided
    And the big black bus decided
    To stop.

MONA: I'm standing on the street.

HETTIE: You're dripping in the heat.

*MONA falters.*

MONA: I can't.

HETTIE: Not much further.

MONA: I can't!

HETTIE: You're running down the street
    And you're dripping in the heat

MONA: Hettie. No.

HETTIE: The bus is long gone
    But still you run on
    Still you run on as the band played on.

MONA: Stop. Wait.

HETTIE: Too late.
    Here we are at the gate.

*MONA's eyes meet LENNY's for the first time.*

MONA: Lenny.

*Pause.*

You like the dress I put on for you?

HETTIE: A simple cotton dress with straps. And him?

MONA: And you? A blue suit. Navy blue.

HETTIE: Double buttons on the sleeve
    I believe.

MONA: White cotton shirt, top button undone just
    enough…

*Silence.*

HETTIE: (*Gently.*) Go on…

MONA: I didn't need to say anything else. He could see it
    in my eyes.

(*Whispers.*) 'Lets go to bed' they said.
'Let's go to bed'.

*Beat.*

Our fingers urged, our bodies merged. And then…and
then…and then again….

*Pause.*

You were right, Lenny. We were good at it.

*MONA's hand touches her stomach lightly.*

I should have told you she was there. I know I should.
But I didn't want that moment to break. I felt alive. I
felt…

*MONA looks to HETTIE –*

HETTIE / MONA: Complete.

*Pause. MONA winces.*

MONA: Lenny?

*MONA clutches her stomach in pain.*

(*Screaming.*) Lenny!

HETTIE: (*Gently.*) Ssh….

MONA: Lenny!

HETTIE: Sshhhhhhh……

*Silence.*

MONA: Describe her to me.

LENNY: What?

MONA: Do you ever imagine what she would look like?

LENNY: She?

MONA: Do you?

LENNY: Do you?

*Beat.*

MONA: How tall would she be?

LENNY: Does it matter?

MONA: No. How tall?

LENNY: Tall. Like me.

MONA: No. Petite. Like me. Eyes?

LENNY: Brown.

MONA: Black. Hair?

LENNY: Curly.

MONA: Straight. Fingers?

LENNY: Long?

MONA: Chubby.

HETTIE: Chubby?

MONA: Chubby.

HETTIE: Says who?

MONA: Says me.

LENNY: Mona.

*Beat.*

Who are you talking to?

*Pause.*

MONA: And there's my Father standing there, his eyes cold as the grave. 'There's nothing I can say, Mona. You made your bed.' He didn't punish me with the switch. He punished me with silence. But I knew what he was thinking. My little girl. Doing *that*.

The tears were welling up inside. 'No. Not now. Not like this.' Forcing themselves up from the depths of my shame. And all the time him just standing there. 'I have nothing to say, Mona. Nothing.'

The air was thick with foul language as I gave voice to my shame. Filth pouring from my mouth, prodding him in the chest with my finger.

*MONA jabs the air –*

There! There! There!

The only time I had ever touched my father was when he held my hand to take me to school, but here I was making free wid 'im body, cussin' like a fishwife. Prodding and jabbing like I was checking the meat at the market.

*She jabs –*

There! Nothing

*Again –*

There! Nothing.

*She raises her finger to jab again –*

And then it happened.

*Beat.*

His voice seemed to claw its way up from the pit of his stomach. I was terrified, but I couldn't stop –

*She jabs –*

There! Yes!

*Again-*

There! Yes!

He was screaming at me, cussing *with* me, meeting my anger with his. Alive and out of control. *Good!* I broke him down. *Good!* It's not just me. *Good!* I'M NOT ALONE!

*Beat.*

The room went dark, just for a second. Then light. Much brighter than before and I felt as light as the air around me. So light that, as I staggered backwards, I allowed myself to float towards the ground. As my cheek brushed the floor my father's face came into view. He knelt beside me. Kissed my tender cheek. Whispered his apologies. His eyes wide. Terrified. Full of fear and wonder.

*Beat.*

I had won. And he knew it.

LENNY: Did you feel better?

MONA: Of course I felt better. That's the beauty of winning. You can be wrong and still win.

*From the depths of her soul MONA lets out a cry of anguish. It hangs in the air –*

It. Hurts.

LENNY: I know.

MONA: I need you to remember, so I don't have to do it on my own. Please –

*A tiny smile creeps across LENNY's face.*

LENNY: Sorry.

*LENNY turns.*

MONA: Where are you going?

LENNY: Home.

MONA: And leaving me here?

LENNY: You live here. Remember?

MONA: I'm sorry. Alright? I'm sorry.

*LENNY goes to the door.*

You can't leave me here! Please Lenny.

HETTIE: (*Mocking.*) Please, Lenny.

MONA: I'm beggin' you. You can't leave me here with her!

LENNY: Who?

MONA: She's standing right in front of you!

*Pause.*

LENNY: There's no-one here.

*Pause.*

Except you.

*Silence.*

MONA: And you?

*A smile creeps across LENNY's face.*

LENNY: Me?

*Pause. MONA is struck with a terrible realisation – She backs away from LENNY.*

MONA: Get away… Get away from me –

LENNY: What?

MONA: Stay away from me!

LENNY: Mona –

MONA: I said stay away from me!

LENNY: Calm down.

MONA: Shut up! Shut up don't say anything.

LENNY: Or what? What are you going to do?

MONA: I'll – I'll –

LENNY: You'll what?

MONA: I – I – I – I –

LENNY: Sorry. Not quite catching that –

MONA: I'm calling the police!

LENNY: No phone. Remember?

MONA: I know what you're trying to do. I know –

*LENNY moves towards MONA.*

MONA: I said stay away from me!

LENNY: Will you please calm down.

MONA: You're doing this –

LENNY: What?

MONA: You're doing this to me –

LENNY: I think that says more about you than it does about me. It's called paranoia.

*Pause.*

MONA: Get out!

LENNY: Fine –

MONA: No –

LENNY: What? Go. Stay. Go. Stay. This behaviour is completely irrational.

MONA: I'm not irrational. You do this to me. You make me feel like this.

LENNY: Like I made you sleep with me?

MONA: Why won't you help me?

LENNY: Why should I?

MONA: Because I'm losing my mind!

*Pause.*

LENNY: (*Gently.*) Well. A break*down* is a break*through*.

MONA: What?

LENNY: Maybe we're finally getting somewhere. You can fight it. Or you can take a good long look at yourself. Denial is an important part of the healing process. That's just where you are right now.

MONA: No. You see, I know. And I know you. I know you can see her. You just want to torment me. You made her come. You made her follow me didn't you?

LENNY: Will you just listen to yourself for a minute?

MONA: No! No I will not listen to myself!

LENNY: Then listen to me.

*Pause.*

There's no-one else here.
You're seeing things that aren't there.

*Beat.*

You're losing your mind.
You're losing your looks.
You're old, bitter and vindictive, but most importantly,
you're alone.

*Beat.*

You've wasted your life, and for what?

*Beat.*

You have no children of your own and you never will.
You couldn't even keep a child, let alone a man –
Married? Us?
Just one pussy for the rest of my life?
Just one pussy then I take she for wife?
I don't think so.

*Beat.*

I never loved you.
I just wanted to sleep with you.

*Beat.*

Now? I wouldn't shit on you.

*Silence.*

MONA: Finished?

LENNY: Yes.

MONA: Feels better doesn't it?

LENNY: Yes.

MONA: Just for a moment.

LENNY: Yes.

*Pause.*

MONA: Just for a moment…

*Pause.*

And now?

*Silence. LENNY falters –*

LENNY: And now I'm watching the woman that I thought was the sexiest, most vibrant, intelligent, beautiful woman I have ever known fade before me eyes. And it's breaking my heart. You need me to remember, but I don't.

MONA: There's no comfort here.

LENNY: No. I took the easy option. I drank to forget.

*Beat.*

It worked.

*Beat.*

I'm sorry.

*Silence.*

MONA: When did I become – ? Have I always been so – ?

*Beat.*

What will I do?

LENNY: I don't know.

*LENNY turns to leave.*

I'll call someone.

MONA: What will they do?

*Pause.*

LENNY: Is she still here?

MONA: Yes.

*LENNY presses his fingers into his eyes, desperate to hold back the tears.*

Please don't. I deserve it.

LENNY: (*Gently.*) Still playing the martyr?

MONA: (*The faintest of smiles.*) Yes. And we all know what happens to martyrs.

*LENNY moves slowly to the door.*

When you get home. Don't take AJ swimming anymore. Try football.

*Pause.*

I can't do this on my own. I can't. Cope.

LENNY: Step One.

*LENNY exits. MONA and HETTIE face each other in silence as the lights fade.*

9 781840 025019